Football's
CRUSHING
BLOCKERS

Oakland's All-Pro guard Gene Upshaw takes a break during the Raiders' 32-14 thrashing of the Vikings in Super Bowl XI.

The SPORTS HEROES Library

Football's CRUSHING BLOCKERS

Nathan Aaseng

Lerner Publications Company · Minneapolis

To Matt

LIBRARY OF CONGRESS CATALOGING IN PUBLICATION DATA

Aaseng, Nathan.
Football's crushing blockers.

(The Sports heroes library)
Summary: A collective biography of football's "unsung
heroes," such as Gene Upshaw, Jim Langer, Dan Dierdorf,
and others.

1. Football players—United States—Biography—Juvenile literature. 2. Blocking (Football)—Juvenile literature.
[1. Football players] I. Title. II. Series.

GV939.A1A163   796.332'092'2 [B] [920]   81-13681
ISBN 0-8225-1074-X   AACR2

Manufactured in the United States of America

International Standard Book Number: 0-8225-1074-X
Library of Congress Catalog Card Number: 81-13681

2 3 4 5 6 7 8 9 10 91 90 89 88 87 86 85 84 83

Contents

The Steelers' thickly muscled center Mike Webster holds off an Oiler lineman.

Introduction

Jerry Kramer, who played offensive guard for the Green Bay Packers, once said that if he ever had to hide from the law, he would go back to being an offensive lineman. There may be no better way for an outstanding pro athlete to stay unnoticed than by playing blocker in pro football. When a running back scores on a long run, he gets credit for the yards and the points. But the blocker who made the run possible is completely ignored. In fact, the offensive lineman is only noticed when he makes a mistake! Even in the thickest books of football statistics there is only one category for individual offensive linemen, and that is for penalties.

Mike Kenn of the Atlanta Falcons is a good example of the no-win situation faced by blockers. Kenn not only blocked well in 1980, he went the entire season without committing a single penalty.

Guard John Hannah paves the way for a New England runner.

But because he was never cited for a penalty, his name was almost never mentioned during a game. Although he helped his team to the play-offs, Kenn, who earned All-Pro ratings from the players, was one of football's best-kept secrets that year.

A blocker's job, however, used to be even worse than it is today. For many years, blockers were not allowed to use their hands at all. It was all they could do to protect themselves from the helmet-slapping and the grabbing of the defensive linemen. But in 1979, the linemen were finally given a break. Then headslaps were made illegal, and blockers were allowed some use of their hands. Since those changes were made, defenses have found it much harder to dominate their opponents.

There are five positions on the offensive line. The center lines up directly over the ball. He must be able to hike the ball to the quarterback while getting himself set to block a tackle or a middle linebacker. This difficult job calls for quickness as well as enough strength to take on the huge nose tackles. The two guards line up on either side of the center. They are usually slightly larger than the center. Quickness is not quite as important to a guard as to a center, but the guards must be fast enough to lead the way on end sweeps. They work

9

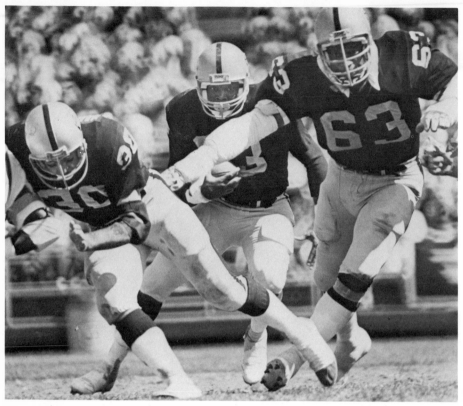

Raider running back Kenny King (33) looks for an opening behind blocks by Gene Upshaw and Mark van Eeghen (30).

with the center in protecting the quarterback from pass rushers trying to break through the middle of the line. The outside posts on the line are manned by the tackles. These are usually huge, powerful men who can shove the defensive ends to one side or the other on both running and passing plays.

Blocking for a pass is completely different than blocking for a run. On a run, the blocker charges forward and drives his man backwards or to one side. It is his chance to attack and open up room for the runners. But when a pass play is called, the blocker is more concerned about keeping his opponent away from the quarterback than about moving him backwards. Always careful to shield the quarterback with his body, he slowly gives ground and reacts to the defensive man's moves.

Although the offensive lineman's job sounds simple, it is really one of the most difficult in pro football. Even the most talented blockers usually need two or three years to learn their technique and how to work with their fellow blockers. Linemen must be more patient and disciplined than other players in order to succeed at their position.

While fans may not notice offensive linemen, the defenses certainly do. In a 1969 game against the New York Jets, the Minnesota Vikings tried to run an end sweep. Their guards got their directions mixed up, however. One ran to the left, the other to the right—and they crashed into each other. On the other side of the line, the Jets linebackers were each watching a lineman to see which way the play would go. Two of *them* sprinted in opposite directions, and *they* knocked each other down! That freak play showed that defensive players often watch the blockers more closely than they do the ball. They know that the key to tackling the ball carrier is first to get around the blockers.

Football coaches also appreciate the thankless job that their offensive linemen perform. They know that the outcome of a game often depends upon which side controls the line of scrimmage. When the offensive line is in control, the running backs find room to run, and the quarterback has time to find an open receiver. Here are eight players who have often controlled the line of scrimmage and have made stars of their running backs and quarterbacks.

1
Gene Upshaw
GUARD

The Oakland Raiders were in deep trouble in the 1977 Super Bowl. A crowd of over 100,000 fans seemed to be leaning over their shoulders as Oakland huddled in their own end zone, planning their next move. The Raiders had the ball on their own six-yard line, third down and seven yards to go for a first down. Somehow they had to move the ball far enough on the next play to give their punter room to kick. But even then, the Minnesota Vikings would get the ball in good field position in this scoreless game.

Quarterback Ken Stabler decided to put his trust in his giant linemen on the left side, Gene Upshaw and Art Shell. The ball was hiked, and Upshaw drove Alan Page out of the way. Shell did the same to Jim Marshall. Running back Clarence Davis then picked his way past the fallen bodies for 35 yards and a first down. That was the turning point of the game, and the Raiders went on to win, 32-14. Those who followed Oakland closely were not surprised to find Gene Upshaw in the middle of this important play. The veteran guard had always seemed to play a key role in important Raider games.

Gene was born in 1945 in the southern Texas town of Robstown. There he received early training in battling pro linemen when he competed with his younger brother, Marvin. Marvin later faced Gene across the line of scrimmage as a defensive end for Oakland's arch-rival, the Kansas City Chiefs.

Gene did not attract any scholarship offers from colleges, so he attended Texas A&I University in nearby Kingsville. There he played center, tackle, and end on the football team, and he kept in shape by putting the shot for the track team. When it came to football, Texas A&I, a school of about 7,000, was far overshadowed by its bigger Texas rival, Texas A&M. But the Oakland Raiders had scouted the swift 260-pounder, and they had decided he was good enough to rate their first round draft choice in 1967.

Even in that first year, Upshaw played like a

Gene Upshaw

seasoned professional and made crucial contribu-
tions to the team. That year the Raiders advanced
to the play-offs against the Houston Oilers. Early
in the game, Oakland faced a third and six situation
on their own 31-yard line. Upshaw leveled his
opponent with a block, springing fullback Hewritt
Dixon loose for 69 yards and a touchdown. Sparked
by that play, the Raiders won easily and advanced
to the Super Bowl.

Although it was a thrill for Gene to start in a Super Bowl as a rookie, it was also a disappointing experience. Oakland lost, 33-14, to the Green Bay Packers. That loss was the first of many frustrating moments for Gene as the Raiders often came close to winning the title, only to fail in the end.

Learning his trade more quickly than most linemen, Gene was voted All-Pro in 1968. That was an honor he was to earn six more times in the next seasons—in 1969, 1970, 1971, 1972, 1974, and 1977. In 1970 Upshaw was joined on the left side by mammoth tackle Art Shell, whose weight has been estimated at anywhere from 275 to 300 pounds. Upshaw and Shell provided the power for Oakland's left-handed attack, a style that made it comfortable for their left-handed passer, Ken Stabler.

Because they were more interested in wins than in records, the Raider line rarely led the conference in protecting the passer. Most teams expected their quarterback to pass the ball within three seconds after it was hiked. But the Raiders asked their linemen to provide *four* seconds of protection to allow them to run deep pass patterns. Because of this extra demand, Stabler was sacked a few more times than some other quarterbacks. But he was usually able to wait until his receivers had broken clear, and he became the league's most accurate passer.

On running plays, the Raiders used an old-fashioned, straight-ahead style of power football. While this did not produce many exciting runs, it did allow Oakland to use up the clock on safe, steady drives. Again it took an exceptional group of blockers to succeed at that kind of attack.

But Upshaw not only proved to be Oakland's top blocker. He also gave them such fearless leadership that he was named the offensive captain in 1973. Brimming with confidence, Gene wanted each game to start with a simple running play. That would give him a chance to push back his opponent and to show him that he was in for a long afternoon. Upshaw cleared such huge holes for his backs in the 1970s that his side of the line became known as "Highway 63" after his jersey number. Runners such as Mark Van Eeghen, who rushed for over 1,000 yards in three straight years, knew they could count on their big left guard. Despite knee and back problems, the durable Upshaw started in over 200 straight games.

In 1976 Oakland finally got revenge on the Pittsburgh Steelers, the team that had beaten them in the conference championship two years in a row. With Upshaw leading the way, the Raiders ran through the famed Steeler defense for 157 yards rushing in a 24-7 win.

Two weeks later, Oakland faced the Minnesota Vikings in the Super Bowl. Some of the Vikings later commented that the Raider linemen seemed so huge they blotted out the sun. And they certainly kept the sun from shining on the Vikings in that game. Oakland ran 17 of their 20 first-half running plays behind Shell and Upshaw, who opened enough holes in the defense to give Oakland a 16-10 lead. Before the afternoon was over, the Raiders had piled up 266 yards running. Halfback Davis had dashed through the Vikings for 137 on only 16 carries in the Raiders' 32-14 win.

Because of Oakland's reputation as an unfriendly bunch of brawlers, many claimed that the game was a "victory for the bad guys." But Upshaw was one Raider who did not fit that description—at least not off the field. He won the 1980 Byron White Award, which was given to the player who had done the most for community service. Gene had worked for so many organizations that the list rivaled the Yellow Pages. Even during the season, he rarely found an evening when he was not involved in some worthwhile cause. Gene said that was his way

Upshaw launches into a block against San Diego.

of showing appreciation for what he had been given in life.

The San Diego Chargers were one team that wished Gene had shown them as much consideration as he had shown his community. In the 1980 American Football Conference championship game, the Chargers had rallied from far behind to draw within a touchdown of Oakland. With over six minutes left in the game, there was plenty of time

Behind the protection of Upshaw and the rest of the Raider offensive line, quarterback Jim Plunkett passes against the Eagles in Super Bowl XV.

for the Chargers to get the ball back for their explosive offense. Charger fans screamed their support as the San Diego defense took the field. With three All-Pros—Fred Dean, Gary Johnson, and Lou Kelcher—digging in on the Charger front line, it seemed foolish for Oakland to try to overpower them with straight-ahead running plays. But Upshaw and his friends drove back the Chargers time after time. Oakland gained so many first downs that San Diego never got the ball again during that game!

That 34-27 win against the Chargers sent the 35-year-old Upshaw into his third Super Bowl game. This time the Philadelphia Eagles, who had sacked Oakland's quarterback eight times a few weeks earlier, were favored to win. But Upshaw's line stopped the Eagle rush and allowed only one sack. The rest of the time quarterback Jim Plunkett had enough time to pick apart the Philadelphia defense in a 27-10 win. And as usual, one of the backfield men, Plunkett, won the Most Valuable Player Award. But just as typically, Gene Upshaw had quietly been a key factor in yet another Raider win.

As Dolphin quarterback Bob Griese drops back into the pocket,
Jim Langer looks for pass rushers to block.

2

Jim Langer

CENTER

Jim Langer started playing football on a very small scale. Born in 1948 in Little Falls, Minnesota, he grew up in the nearby community of Royalton. He was one of the 14 boys who made up the entire Royalton High School football team. Some of his high school games were played on fields that still had corn stalks standing in them.

In this setting, it was easy to see why the three-sport star was overlooked by the major colleges. After graduation, Langer ended up at South Dakota State University instead of at a larger school. There he found time to wrestle, pitch baseball, play football, study, and work his way through school.

Baseball had always been Jim's favorite sport. A left-hander with a fine knuckleball, he posted a

13-1 record at South Dakota State one year. Oddly, it was a football injury that forced him to give up baseball and to concentrate on football instead. As a middle linebacker, his arm was constantly giving and receiving hits. This had built up a deposit of calcium in his arm that made it hard for him to throw a baseball.

At the end of his college career in 1970, Langer was not drafted by any pro team. But Jim persuaded the Cleveland Browns to give him a tryout, and he impressed them enough to make the reserve squad. Langer was thrilled at the chance to be a pro, and he hardly dared to hope for anything more in his career.

Later that year, Jim was sold to the Miami Dolphins. At Miami, head coach Don Shula and offensive line coach Monte Clarke were putting together a remarkable group of blockers. They took unimpressive cast-offs, such as Langer, Larry Little, and Wayne Moore—none of whom had been drafted—and formed them into a strong unit.

At 6 feet, 2 inches, and 250 pounds, Langer was one of the smallest Miami blockers. But he was strong with a sturdy 19-inch neck, quick feet, and a no-nonsense approach to practice. The Dolphins tried him at guard and center, and he won a reserve

Jim Langer

role with them. In one 1971 win over the Chicago Bears, Langer played four different offensive line positions. But he spent most of his time learning how to play center from veteran Bob DeMarco.

Two things made Langer an unusual center from the start. First, even though he was left-handed, he snapped the ball with his right hand. This gave him a chance to use his strong left arm quickly for blocking. Secondly, he lined up over the ball with his knees locked like a guard's rather than bent.

Langer does battle against a big Kansas City Chief.

Jim felt this gave him a more powerful drive on straight-ahead plays.

Langer worked himself into a starting role in 1972. He performed tirelessly and stayed in for more plays than most centers. It is hard for a center to protect himself from a lineman's charge while concentrating on long snaps for punts and field goals. Most teams do not risk their starting center for such chores. But Langer wanted to become an all-around player, so he learned to handle the long snaps as well. He also stayed in the game for kickoff returns.

Perhaps Jim's most noticeable performance was on a kickoff in 1974 against the Oakland Raiders. Langer knocked down one Raider. Then he got up and bowled over another with a clean shot. That gave Nat Moore enough room to run the kick for a touchdown.

Besides playing more than most football players, Jim also took more punishment. The Dolphins played in hot weather on an artificial surface. While the other players could wear padding to protect themselves from turf burns, Langer had to have his hands free to control the hike.

Langer not only survived the Miami heat, he developed into a great player. Quarterback Bob Griese was given much credit for masterminding

Miami's running attack, but Langer was behind it, too. It was his job to call out blocking assignments for various formations. Jim and his teammates did their jobs so well that in the mid-1970s the Dolphin ground game was nearly unstoppable.

The Dolphins' control of the line was a main ingredient in their undefeated season in 1972. In that season's Super Bowl, Miami blocked well and helped fullback Larry Csonka churn out yards through the middle of the line in a 14-7 win over the Washington Redskins.

The next season, the Dolphins earned a 12-2 record and again coasted through the play-offs into the Super Bowl. This time Langer, Larry Little, and Bob Kuechenberg dominated the middle of the Minnesota Vikings' defense so well that the Dolphins rarely had to resort to a pass. The blocking unleashed Csonka for a Super Bowl record of 145 yards, mostly on plays straight up the middle. The Dolphins won easily, 24-7, with Csonka singled out as the game's Most Valuable Player.

Langer enjoyed four straight years—from 1973 to 1977—as the league's top center. Despite his big league success, however, he was still a small-town person at heart. He had become fed up with Miami's heat and drugs and with city life in general.

In 1978 he began to warn the Dolphins that he would rather retire than stay in the city much longer. Langer, however, was so valuable that the Dolphins would not think of trading him.

Jim kept up his fine performance until October 1979. Then in a game in which Jim and his mates thrashed the Green Bay Packers, Jim suffered a chipped bone in his knee. That injury sidelined him for the rest of the year.

The next year found Jim back in Minnesota, working in a bank and tending to his small, 45-acre farm. He insisted that he would not play ball anymore unless he could play for the nearby Vikings. Minnesota already had a fine young center, Dennis Swilley, but it could not afford to pass up a chance to get Langer at a cheap price. So they sent two middle-round draft picks to Miami and welcomed Langer to the team.

After the trade, Jim claimed that he was the luckiest player in the game. He owned two Super Bowl rings, and he could finish his career playing close to home. That was a well-earned bit of fortune for Jim who, before retiring prior to the 1982 season, had worked hard to turn himself from an unwanted, small college player into what Don Shula called "the best center in the history of pro football."

A ferocious-looking Dan Dierdorf gets into his pass-blocking stance.

3
Dan Dierdorf
TACKLE

There are few tougher tasks in football than that of the offensive tackle on pass plays. Then the tackle is usually forced to fend off a charging defensive end all by himself. He must stand his ground against those bruising defensive linemen, absorbing blow after blow. With just one slip, a defensive end will shoot past and tackle the quarterback for a large loss. And if the offensive team is forced to pass a lot, the tackle must keep warding off those attacks without ever getting a chance to get in his own licks.

Yet somehow tackle Dan Dierdorf always made it look as though *he* was the one on the attack. Dierdorf, who stood 6 feet, 3 inches tall and was listed at 288 pounds, came to about 320 pounds when he put on his St. Louis Cardinal uniform and

Dan Dierdorf

equipment. And Dierdorf knew how to throw that weight around! Even the greatest defensive ends have spent most of their games against St. Louis bouncing off Dan as if he were a cement slab.

Dan was born in 1949 in Canton, Ohio, the birthplace of pro football. It was not the town but the state that put the most pressure on him, however. As a standout high school lineman, Dierdorf was expected to play for one of the football-mad Ohio colleges, such as Ohio State. So he was considered almost a traitor when he left the state to enroll at arch-rival University of Michigan. But Dan was convinced that he could get the coaching he needed at Michigan.

Dierdorf started as an offensive tackle for the Michigan Wolverines for three straight years. From his two years of playing alongside All-American tight end Jim Mandich, who later starred with the Miami Dolphins, he learned a good deal about blocking. He also learned how to relax before Saturday games by watching the early morning cartoons. With halfback Billy Taylor following Dierdorf for long runs, Michigan went undefeated in the 1970 regular season, only to lose to Stanford, 13-12, in the Rose Bowl.

Dan's performance that year made him the "yardstick" by which all other college tackles were measured. "He's almost as good as Dierdorf," became one of the highest compliments a young tackle could receive. The St. Louis Cardinals could not help but notice all the players Dan had knocked down in his college career. So they were thrilled that he was still available in the second round of the 1971 draft, and they claimed him for their team.

Like many college linemen, Dierdorf knew little

about pass blocking. After all, his college team had only used the pass to give their running backs a rest. It took him a full season to begin to catch on to the art of protecting the passers. But the following year, 1972, he made such progress that he was voted the Cardinals' Most Improved Player.

Dan quickly became the main man in the National Football League's top pass-blocking line. Along with scrappy Conrad Dobler and powerful Bob Young at guards and wildman Tom Banks at center, Dan helped to make Cardinal quarterback Jim Hart the most worry-free passer in football. Hart found plenty of time to drop back, look over the defense, and wait until speedy receivers such as Mel Gray broke loose from the defense. Hart was so well protected from combat that at times he must have thought he was playing touch instead of tackle football!

When he started up a "kitty," Dierdorf helped the Cardinal line to work as a team. Any offensive lineman who made a mistake, such as a penalty, or who allowed a sack had to pay into the kitty. Dierdorf's teammates took up the challenge so well that there was never much money changing hands. From 1972 to 1977, quarterback Hart was sacked an average of only 13 times per season, or about 1 per game! The Cardinal line led the entire NFL in preventing sacks three straight years and in their conference for five straight years.

The Cardinals' most incredible performance of all came in 1975. That year quarterback Hart was caught behind the line only six times, and the Cardinals won their divisional title. During that time, it was Dierdorf who shouldered the heaviest load as he shielded Hart from the most feared pass rushers in the game. Defensive ends Jack Youngblood of Los Angeles, Carl Eller of Minnesota, and Claude Humphrey of Atlanta all drew Dan as their opponent on the line, and none of them had much success.

Dan also proved that he was *more* than a pass blocker. He took advantage of his chances to charge into the defense, leading the way for Terry Metcalf and Jim Otis. Though Otis was not considered an outstanding back, he managed to find enough room in 1975 to lead the entire National Football Conference with 1,076 yards.

Dan had always been most impressed with those players who came through with steady performances, game in and game out. He worked so hard at achieving steadiness that, since becoming a regular in 1971, he never had a poor season. Dan was voted to the Pro Bowl every year from 1974 to 1978, and he would have continued his streak had he not

Dierdorf blocks the Eagles' Mel Tom out of a Cardinal running play.

been severely injured in 1979. And starting in 1976, Dan had been named the top lineman in the National Football Conference for *three* years in a row!

Dierdorf is one of those people who was probably as well known in St. Louis for his activities off the field as on. He was very active in all kinds of community projects as well as in business, and he operated a swimming pool company and a radio show.

But despite his many football accomplishments, Dierdorf rarely received any publicity. It was almost unbelievable that a man so large and skilled as he could escape notice. Dan has never even been voted the Most Valuable Player on his *team*. But he shrugged off his lack of fame. "I outgrew the running back position long ago," he laughs. Besides, the people he plays against know how good he is. Anyone who has ever had to play one-on-one with Dierdorf for 60 minutes was not likely to forget him.

A Patriot ball carrier waits for guard John Hannah to crush a Bronco linebacker.

4
John Hannah
GUARD

On game days, the New England Patriots love to have guard John Hannah as their teammate. But during the rest of the week, they are not so sure it is a blessing to have him around. "Hog" Hannah is football's most ferocious offensive lineman. And he never lets up, no matter if it is in the middle of a close game or in the the last minute of an ordinary practice. Teammates and opponents who value their health do their best to keep away from that hard-charging All-Pro.

John's drive to succeed at football started shortly after he was born in Canton, Georgia, in 1951. John's father spent part of that year playing football for the New York Giants. Unfortunately, the pay was not as good as it is today, and his dad had to give up football after only one year in order to support his family. But he loved to talk about that one season and the career he might have had if he had been born later. John listened eagerly to those stories and hoped that he, too, would get his chance at a pro career.

From an early age, John treated football as if it were a job rather than a game. His first chance to prepare for his pro career came in the fourth grade. But even though he was large and a very hard worker, he was not very strong. For years he was pushed around on the football field. Even in high school in Albertville, Alabama, John was called "Fatso" by his classmates. But by the time he was ready for college, his body had developed into a perfect build for a lineman. With the power from his 34-inch thighs and huge lower body, he had become a fearsome blocker.

John attended the "family" college, the University of Alabama. His father, uncle, and his two brothers had all played football for the Crimson Tide of Alabama, and their wishbone running attack was perfect for a lineman like John. Since their offense rarely used the pass, Hannah merely had to charge into his defensive opponent on every play. Whoever played against John quickly found that Hannah ran on only one speed—full. Hannah once played a game at Tennessee when the temperature on the playing field rose to 120 degrees. Only a player as stubborn and as determined as Hannah would refuse to come out for a rest. He collapsed on the field and nearly lost his life from heat exhaustion.

By the end of his college career, John was as well known to pro scouts as he was to some very sore college opponents, and the All-American guard was the fourth man chosen in the entire 1973 draft of college talent. The floundering New England Patriots claimed him, hoping he could help turn around their desperate blocking situation. Patriot quarterback Jim Plunkett had been getting so battered by defensive pass rushers that his career was in danger.

Hannah became an instant starter for New England, but he did little to improve the offensive line that first year. He tried too hard to be one of the guys, and he fell into some bad training habits that started to affect his life and his play. But he quickly settled down to become one of football's top linemen.

In 1976 Hannah was named as a starter in the Pro Bowl game for the top players in pro football. It had been five years since any Patriot had been

John Hannah

invited to play in the game. At that contest, John learned that he was not making as much money as the other offensive guards. Along with teammate Leon Gray, he walked out of the Patriots' camp the next summer and missed two games before the contract trouble was cleared up.

With Hannah and Gray back for the full year in 1978, the Patriots displayed a high-scoring attack. The linemen cleared the way for fullback Sam Cunningham and company to gain a total of 3,165 yards—more than any NFL team had ever rushed before in a single season. And Hannah gained widespread acclaim as an overwhelming blocker. In one game against the Philadelphia Eagles, Hannah was leading the way on an end sweep. He escorted his runner past the line of scrimmage and into the Philadelphia defensive backfield, where a safety came up to stop the play. The Eagle safety, however, had instructions *not* to challenge Hannah head on. So he gave little resistance, and the runner went on to complete a long gain. The Eagles figured it was better to give up 30 yards than to risk losing their safety in a collision with Hannah!

Despite the Patriots' explosive offense, the team failed to advance in the play-offs in 1979. Football experts that year had a hard time figuring out what was wrong with New England. For several years the Patriots had seemed to have the most talent of any team in the league. Yet they had not come close to earning a spot in the Super Bowl. Several times they missed making the play-offs after crumbling in a key game with a poor team. So the critics started to wonder if there was something wrong with the attitude of the New England players.

But during that time, nobody dared fault the effort of Hannah. The 6-foot, 2-inch, 265-pound

From his three-point stance on the line, Hannah listens to the quarterback's signals before the ball is snapped.

blocker refused to sit out any offensive plays, even if the Patriots had a comfortable lead. Even in practice he was always so fired up that his teammates tried to joke with him to keep him from brooding.

Hannah, however, often played so hard that his temper would sometimes get the best of him. In one game against Minnesota, he was called for a penalty against the Vikings' Alan Page. Hannah thought Page should have been called for the penalty instead, and he became so angry that he started swinging. But he only hurt his team by getting thrown out of the game. That quick temper also caused him to blast some of his teammates at times for not giving a full effort. Even his employers have not been safe from stinging comments from their star guard. John exploded when he heard that his friend Leon Gray had been traded in 1979, and he claimed that he could not wait to finish the remaining years on his contract so he could get out of New England, too.

Hannah later admitted that his temper had been a problem, and he promised that he would try hard to control it. And to hear coaches talk, John's temper might be his only fault as a football player. John Madden, who coached the Oakland Raiders to a Super Bowl win in 1977, was once asked which pro player he would most like to have on his team. His answer was John Hannah.

Opposing players agree that Hannah in action is something to behold. Denver's middle linebacker, Randy Gradishar, remarked that there was no more powerful player in the game than Hannah. So although the fans are busy watching the quarterback, the defense is keeping close track of where big number 73 is going.

Wearing a jersey ripped from the struggles on the field, Leon Gray rests on the sidelines while getting instructions from a Patriot coach in the pressbox.

46

5
Leon Gray
TACKLE

When Leon Gray reported to the Houston Oilers' training camp just before the 1979 season, doctors swarmed over him, as curious as if he were a mummy come to life. They examined him closely, trying to find out what was wrong with him. But instead they found nothing but a large, powerful man in perfect health. Somehow that made no sense. Why would New England trade a young All-Pro tackle unless something was wrong with him?

That was a question that baffled football fans, too, especially those in New England. There *was* nothing wrong with Leon Gray. Yet the Patriots weakened their title chances by giving up a great player for a draft choice. Since the trade, Gray's performance has proven how big a mistake they had made.

Leon was born in Memphis, Tennessee, in 1951, and he grew up in rural Olive Branch, Mississippi. He could hardly have had a more discouraging start to his football career. As a boy, Leon was so short and fat that he was run off the football team. But Gray was determined to earn his way through college somehow. If he could not get an athletic scholarship, then he would try for another kind of scholarship. So he worked hard at his studies and at music. After long hours of practice, he became an excellent trumpet player.

Leon started growing, though, and by his high school days, he was enormous. But now the football team had to get *him* to join *them.* Gray did, but he kept up his interest in music, too. He even marched with the band during halftimes of the football games, wearing his football gear.

The studying paid off for Gray when he earned an academic scholarship to Jackson State University in Mississippi. During college he continued growing until he had swelled to 300 pounds. He started all four years at Jackson State, and his size helped him to ward off defensive linemen.

In 1973 the Miami Dolphins snatched him in the third round of the college draft. Leon, unfortunately, could not have found a tougher place to try and break into pro football. The Dolphins were in their prime Super Bowl years, and they had the best offensive line in the game. There simply was no room on the team for a newcomer such as Gray. New England, however, could not afford to be so choosy when it came to blocking help, and they eagerly picked him up from Miami on waivers. At New England, Gray was able to relax and to learn the skills of a pro tackle without having to worry about getting cut from the team.

Midway through the 1973 season, Leon quickly earned a spot in the starting lineup as the left tackle alongside John Hannah. The two soon developed into football's most devastating blocking combination. A poll of National Football League scouts showed how highly the Patriots' left-side blockers were regarded. When asked to name the hardest-hitting players in the game, they came up with a short list that included only two offensive linemen—Gray and Hannah. The two became close friends and were thrilled when both were voted to the Pro Bowl game in 1976.

Their joy, however, quickly turned to anger when they found out how underpaid they were compared to the other All-Stars. The two joined forces again, this time against the management of New England.

Patriot tackle Leon Gray lines up opposite the Raiders' defensive wall and linebacker Ted Hendricks.

It was a tough time for everyone involved when the two linemen missed two regular season games. Finally they were ordered back to work by the players' association, which also criticized the New England management. Although Gray and Hannah blocked well when they returned to the team, it was too late to get New England into the play-offs.

In 1978 the New England powerhouse was rolling. Defensive men were flying like bowling pins, especially when tight end Russ Francis lined up next to Gray and Hannah. The Patriots ground their way into the play-offs, only to lose to Houston in their first game.

By the start of the next season New England's problems seemed to be clearing up, and they appeared to be as strong as ever. Gray was especially eager for the new season. He had shown Patriot fans that he was interested in becoming a part of the New England area when he bought a home there, and he enrolled in a Boston school to finish up his college work. And best of all, his wife was about to give birth to a new son or daughter. Leon had just gone to the hospital with his wife when he got the stunning news. He had been traded to Houston for a number one draft choice.

Football fans were nearly as shocked as Gray was. Rumors said that Leon had slowed down, and that it was only Hannah's reputation that made people think Gray was a good blocker. But the Oilers soon found out the rumors were not true. The 6-foot, 3-inch, 256-pound tackle led the way for Earl Campbell to win the 1979 NFL rushing crown. And he helped Houston battle the Pittsburgh Steelers down to the wire in the AFC championship before losing, 27-14.

In a Texas showdown, Houston's Leon Gray keeps Harvey Martin of the Cowboys away from quarterback Dan Pastorini.

The awards that showered in on Leon further embarrassed his former New England team. He was voted All-Pro, and he also won the Seagram 7 Crown Award in 1979 as football's outstanding lineman. But the best indication of his skill came in comparing quarterback sacks. The Oilers allowed only 11 sacks in their final 13 games of 1979.

Meanwhile the Patriots, operating without Gray, saw their sack total shoot up from 24 in the previous year to 49 in 1979.

The Oilers again drove toward a play-off spot in 1980. They seemed to be well on their way to the Super Bowl when they finally knocked Pittsburgh out of play-off contention with a 6-0 win on December 4. But that game proved to be terribly costly when Gray tore an Achilles' tendon. He could play no more that year, and again the Oilers' dreams of a Super Bowl were dashed. They could not fend off the Oakland Raider pass rushers in the first round of the play-offs and were defeated, 27-7. Houston had become the second team to find out the hard way how valuable Leon Gray was to their team.

By 1982, Leon had become unhappy in Houston. The Oilers had changed coaches the previous season, and their record fell to 7 and 9. Leon and Houston's management could not come to contract terms for the 1982 season, so the Oilers decided to trade him. When they did, Leon joined the New Orleans Saints and his old coach, Bum Phillips. Bum gave up a lot to get Leon—the most popular Saint, quarterback Archie Manning—but, as his former coach, Bum knew very well that a player as rare as Leon is hard to come by at any price.

Buffalo's Joe DeLamielleure gets set to pass block against the Steelers' rush.

6
Joe DeLamielleure
GUARD

The Buffalo Bills' new coach, Lou Saban, did not care what the statistics said. He *knew* that O.J. Simpson was the best running back in football. All that O.J. needed was some blocking and a chance to run, and then he would finally show the world what he could do. So right away in 1972 Saban started to provide blockers for Simpson. With the help of newcomers such as rookie Reggie McKenzie, Simpson won the NFL rushing title that year with 1,251 yards.

The next year, Saban used the draft to collect even more blocking power. He used his first choice to claim Paul Seymour, a tackle from Michigan.

The Bills also had another first round choice from a deal with the Miami Dolphins and selected Joe DeLamielleure, a guard from Michigan State. That choice was the best thing that could have happened to Simpson's career.

Joe was not well known outside of the state of Michigan. He had been born there in 1951, had grown up there, and had played both high school and college football there. As a freshman at Michigan State University, Joe had showed just how serious he was about football when he asked the coaches if he could take a blocking dummy home with him for the summer. The coaches agreed, and the extra practice helped to make DeLamielleure a three-year starter at guard and tackle. Joe was named the Midwest lineman of the week for his blocking against Purdue's 280-pound Dave Butz one week, and he was named All-Big-10 in his final two seasons of college ball. DeLamielleure had also gained just enough of a reputation at Michigan State to earn the chance to play in college all-star games at the end of his senior year. Lou Saban happened to be coaching one of the all-star games. He was so impressed with Joe that he was determined to get him as one of O.J.'s escorts.

Joe's career, however, seemed to be at an end

before he ever suited up for a pro game. While taking a routine physical examination, Joe was found to have a serious heart problem. So the Bills sadly informed Joe that he would have to give up football. DeLamielleure had almost given up hope of playing again when he visited another clinic in Cleveland for further tests. There he happily discovered that his heart was sound enough to play football after all. Joe then took his place as the final link in the great run-blocking line of the Bills.

From the start of the 1973 season, every team knew that Buffalo would run the ball far more than they would throw it. It was no secret that tight end Paul Seymour was not a receiver, but a blocker, and that rookie quarterback Joe Ferguson did not have the pro experience to run a passing attack. Defenses knew that they had only to concentrate on stopping O.J. Simpson to stop the Bills. That fact made it all the more remarkable that Simpson piled up yards at a record pace that year.

By the final game of the season, Simpson was within easy reach of Jim Brown's single season mark of 1,863 yards. But O.J.'s linemen had decided to shoot for an even higher goal against the New York Jets. They wanted him to pass the 2,000-yard level!

As the game went on, the Bill blockers kept

O.J. Simpson credited DeLamielleure and the rest of the Bills offensive line—nicknamed the Electric Company—for much of his success.

closer track of O.J.'s yards than the official scorer did. "Go, Juice!" they said in the huddle after each play. "We gotta get Juice more yards." Early in the first half, Simpson drew within four yards of Brown's record. Then he took a handoff from the quarterback and sprinted to his left. In front of him was Joe DeLamielleure, who had pulled from his right guard spot and was taking aim at a Jet defender barring his path. Joe blocked out the Jet, and Simpson turned upfield, gaining enough yards to break the old record.

The snow started falling in the second half, and the growing darkness brought with it the chilly night air. But the enthusiasm of the Buffalo linemen had not cooled off one bit. Their crushing blocks led O.J. nearer to the 2,000 mark until an off-tackle play in the fourth quarter boosted him to 2,003 yards. After the game, Simpson tried hard to give credit to his linemen. He even brought them with him to interviews on national television.

Even with this unaccustomed exposure, DeLamielleure found himself in the background. For one thing his name (with the accent on the last syllable) was not the simplest to pronounce. It took all of his broad shoulders to fit it on the back of his uniform! But he was also overshadowed by the other guard, Reggie McKenzie. McKenzie was a fine blocker who receive a lot of publicity because he and Simpson were close friends. So with McKenzie in the spotlight, few people knew that Joe DeLamielleure was considered Buffalo's top lineman.

The Bills' line became known as the Electric Company, and they continued to "turn on the Juice" for the next several years. Simpson followed them

DeLamielleure leads a Buffalo running play downfield.

for 1,125 yards in 1974, for 1,817 in 1975, and for 1,503 in 1976, and he won the league rushing title those last two years.

The Bills were one of the few teams during that time that did not tremble at the thought of playing against Pittsburgh's great defensive tackle, Joe Greene. DeLamielleure would line up across from Greene and keep him from doing his usual damage. Though fairly small at 6 feet, 3 inches, and 245 pounds, DeLamielleure was strong, hard-hitting, and fearless, and he would not quit. He also showed fine coordination and quickness—skills which he clearly demonstrated in winning the NFL players' racquetball tournament. Besides all that, Joe survived every Bills' game without a major injury. He was voted All-Pro in 1975, and held onto that honor for six straight seasons.

In the late 1970s, however, Buffalo fell to the bottom of the league standings. They brought in a new head coach, Chuck Knox, who did not get along with Joe. Their troubles grew steadily worse until 1980 when DeLamielleure refused to play any more football for the Bills. He sat out all of the exhibition season, and it seemed his talent would go to waste that year. But on the final day of training camp, the Cleveland Browns gave up a second- and third-round draft choice for his services. Most experts considered it a steal for the Browns.

Joe, however, had built his reputation as a run blocker, and now he had to prove that he could adjust to the pass-happy offense of the Browns.

DeLamielleure in a Cleveland Brown uniform

He quickly worked himself into shape and won a spot on Cleveland's talented offensive line by the season's fourth game. It was more than just a coincidence that Cleveland cut down on the number of quarterback sacks allowed from 43 to 23 that year. With Joe providing key protection, Cleveland's quarterback Brian Sipe went on to win the league's Most Valuable Player Award in 1980. Joe was such a success that he was again voted All-Pro, even though he had missed the first part of the season. It was further proof that, in more ways than one, DeLamielleure was one of the biggest names among pro football linemen.

Husky Pittsburgh center Mike Webster prepares to snap the ball.

7

Mike Webster

CENTER

The Pittsburgh Steelers seemed to have forgotten
to check their weight scales before the 1974 draft
of college players. In the second round, they chose
a linebacker who was considered too light for the
pros. Kent State linebacker Jack Lambert weighed
in at 210 pounds, about the size of a good safety.
Then in the fifth round, they made an even bigger
goof. They chose a 218-pound athlete who was
trained as an offensive lineman. This was not even
close to an acceptable size for a pro center and
even the player, Mike Webster, knew it.

But within four years, the two men had proved
that the Steelers had known what they were doing.
By then they had both become the best at their
positions in the NFL. These two, along with star

receivers Lynn Swann and John Stallworth, made the 1974 Steeler draft one of the best in history. These new players had made the already powerful Steelers the top team in football.

The least known of the new Steeler stars was probably Mike Webster. Mike was born in the north woods Wisconsin town of Tomahawk in 1952. As a boy, he spent so much time working on the family farm and with his dad's construction business that he did not go out for sports. But a powerfully built high school junior could not escape the attention of football coaches for long, especially at a school that needed blocking help as badly as the small high school in nearby Rhinelander.

Mike agreed to join the football team, the wrestling team, and the track team, too. Quickly he made up for his lost years in athletics. During his senior year at Rhinelander, he was voted All-Conference in football on both offense and defense, and his team's Most Valuable Player in football, wrestling *and* track. Although his school was tucked too far in the woods to attract much attention, Mike managed to get a scholarship to attend the University of Wisconsin.

At first Mike had dreams of becoming a hard-tackling linebacker for the Wisconsin Badgers. But those dreams were quickly dashed when he was switched to center. Webster accepted the change, however, and he worked hard and became a three-year starter. Webster, who collectd MVP awards as if they were stamps, added another one during his senior year at Wisconsin when he was voted to the All-Conference team. Most of his efforts paved the way for halfback Bill Marek, who broke school records for rushing yardage. But not even Webster could bring victories to Wisconsin. During Mike's college career, the Badgers never won more than 4 of 11 games in a season.

Webster realized that he was small for a lineman, and he did not expect to be drafted by the pros. But the Pittsburgh Steelers already had a fine veteran center in Ray Mansfield, so they could afford to take a chance on Mike. The Steelers let their fifth-round draft choice wait and learn while Mansfield started for the Super Bowl champs in 1974 and 1975. That was both a good and bad experience for Webster. While he had never been forced to sit on the bench before, he had to admit that it felt good to be on a winning team for the first time in his life.

Webster used his time as a reserve to make use of his weight-lifting hobby. He quickly built himself up to 250 pounds and became recognized as one of the league's strongest men. Webster's upper arms were so large that his uniform sleeves could barely cover them!

When Mansfield retired in 1976, Mike took over at center and kept improving. By 1978 he had taken over Jim Langer's honor as the top center in football. The best example of his progress was his match-up with Curly Culp of the Houston Oilers. Culp was a powerful nose tackle, who lined up just inches from the center's helmet. He gave the Steelers problems every time he played against them, clogging up the middle and knocking over blockers.

At first, Webster needed help from his guards to keep Culp out of the Steeler backfield. But by 1978 he could handle the Oiler nose tackle by himself. In the 1978 and 1979 American Football Conference championships, the Steelers no longer had to worry about the Culp-Webster match-up. Mike controlled his rival from the start, helping his team to a 34-5 win in 1978 and a 27-14 victory the following year.

But Culp was not the only player who failed to dent the Steelers' line. Webster and his fellow weightlifters formed a wall of muscle in front of quarterback Terry Bradshaw. In the 1979 Super Bowl, the Steelers faced the awesome pass rush of

Out in front of quarterback Terry Bradshaw (12) and the rest of the Steeler line, Webster bursts into a Dallas defender during Super Bowl XIII.

the Dallas Cowboys. Cowboy defensive tackle Randy White and defensive end Harvey Martin had torn apart the Denver Bronco passing attack in the previous Super Bowl. But in that game, White found his path blocked by Webster and guard Sam Davis. The Dallas pass rushers were unable to stop Pittsburgh's passing, and Bradshaw had enough time to set a Super Bowl record of four touchdown passes in a 35-31 win.

Having snapped the ball, Webster tries to find an opponent to flatten.

Mike Webster

The following year the Los Angeles Rams challenged the Steelers in the Super Bowl with a smothering defense. For much of the game, the Steelers floundered against the solid Ram defense. Trailing 19-17 in the final quarter, they faced a desperate third and long situation. The Rams knew that the Steelers would have to pass to make a first down on the play, so they turned loose their strong pass rush. But as on every other pass play that day, Bradshaw had time to get the pass off.

He connected with John Stallworth for a 75-yard touchdown to give the Steelers the winning score.

The Steeler-Ram game had been the fourth Super Bowl championship for the young All-Pro center. But he was not about to rest on his success. If there was one thing Mike could not stand, it was a pro athlete who eased up on his effort or complained or acted spoiled. There were no gripes from Webster when he had to hike the ball in freezing rain in a play-off game. He had played most of the 1980 season with injuries, yet he had still made All-Pro. It was all part of the job for Mike, and he felt glad to get a chance to play. And Terry Bradshaw, Franco Harris, and the rest of the Steeler backfield were just as glad that Mike had gotten the chance to play. Because Mike Webster made life a lot happier and safer for the Pittsburgh stars.

8
Marvin Powell
TACKLE

No one could accuse Marvin Powell, Jr., of aiming too low in his life's goals. He spends most of his time with the New York Jets, practicing to become the best offensive tackle in football history. When he is not doing that, he is training to handle the chores as the president of the United States. And if he is as successful at politics as he is at football, he may reach his target of becoming President Powell by 2004.

Powell's father, Marvin, Sr., was an army man. At the age of 15, he had lied about his age to take part in the World War II battle of Normandy. He was stationed at Ft. Bragg, North Carolina, when his son, Marvin, was born in 1955. The elder Powell passed on his enthusiasm about history and world events to his son. By the age of nine, Marvin was reading history and philosophy books and discussing them with his father.

Those discussions were interrupted when Marvin's father was sent to fight in Viet Nam. Then Marvin had to learn to deal with the stress of knowing that his father was in a dangerous situation far from home.

Although he was aware of the dangers of military life, Marvin, Jr., wanted to follow his dad's footsteps into an army career. But instead he got sidetracked by his athletic skill. A football coach at his Lafayette-ville, North Carolina, high school had talked him into going out for football, and Marvin became a fine tight end. His reputation spread all the way to the West Coast, and he attracted offers from colleges such as the University of Southern California. Marvin took Southern Cal's offer and enrolled at the school in 1973.

Even as a freshman, Marvin's intelligence paid off on the football field. He decided that he was not as exceptional at catching a ball as he was at blocking. So he asked the coaches to switch him to the less glamorous position of offensive tackle. The coaches agreed, and Powell moved into the starting lineup on Southern Cal's national champion Trojans

Marvin Powell

in 1974. He was recognized as an All-Pacific Athletic Conference tackle three years in a row. Meanwhile he kept up his other interests by majoring in speech and political science.

Powell was the fourth player and the first lineman chosen in the 1977 draft of college talent. Marvin felt that his excellent training at college could help him become an instant success with the New York

Huge tackle Marvin Powell of the Jets keeps a Raider defender at bay.

Jets, but he was slowed by a knee injury. The following year, it was his ankle that held back his progress.

Still the Jets counted heavily on their young right tackle. In 1978 they drafted a left tackle, 278-pound Chris Ward from Ohio State, and announced that they were going to rebuild the whole offense around their two giant tackles. Powell and Ward became known as the "bookends" who would hold up the Jets' offense.

During the winter after the 1978 season, Marvin made up his mind to become the best tackle in football. As usual he took the mental approach to learning his position. He watched films of such great tackles as Dan Dierdorf and George Kunz to see what he could learn from their techniques. When it came time to report to training camp, Powell was hooked on films. He would watch them for four hours each day, trying to detect weaknesses in himself and in his opponents. Then he would play the upcoming game in his mind, trying to picture what his opponent would do in each situation.

All of this preparation, combined with his tough, overpowering physical play, made Powell a huge success. The Jets, who had never been known for their running attack, surprised everyone by leading the league in rushing. Many of these yards, and most of the important ones, followed paths cleared by the 6-foot, 5-inch, 268-pound Powell. And Marvin was just as tough in protecting young quarterback Richard Todd from pass rushers. For his efforts, he was voted All-Pro and was named the Jets' Most Valuable Player.

After having been chosen by many to win their division, the Jets crash-landed in 1980, finishing 4-12. But Marvin was still at the top of his game.

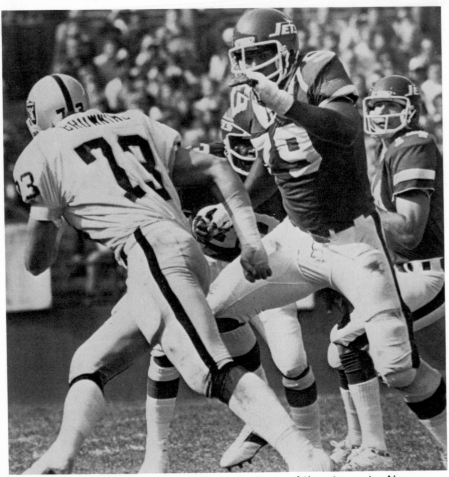

All-Pro Powell gives his quarterback plenty of time to spot a New York receiver downfield.

Again he was selected All-Pro and given a starting position in the Pro Bowl game. After only four years in the league, he had already become the most honored lineman in the history of the Jets.

Marvin showed such total dedication to his job that it was hard to imagine that he had time for anything else. But he was still as much of a bookworm as ever. Thanks to a daily four-hour reading habit, Powell's eyes received as much of a workout as his body. And not all of Powell's reading was done just for fun. Marvin was preparing himself for a career in politics, so he studied biographies, histories, the Bible, and psychology in order to learn about human nature. He also enrolled in law school during the off-season. Powell even dressed the part of a politician and wore suits and ties and carried a brief-case on football road trips.

With his hard work, imagination, and strong back, Powell is convinced that he could make an excellent president some day. And if that is what it takes to be a good president, Marvin Powell will certainly get votes from the National Football League players. They have seen plenty of evidence of those qualities on third-down plays aimed at his tackle spot.

ACKNOWLEDGMENTS: The photographs are reproduced through the courtesy of: pp. 2, 20, 69, Vernon J. Biever; pp. 6, 64, 70, 71, Pittsburgh Steelers; pp. 8, 38, 42, 44, 50, New England Patriots; pp. 10, 15, 19, Oakland Raiders; pp. 22, 25, 26, Miami Dolphins; pp. 30, 32, 36, St. Louis Football Cardinals; p. 46, Mike Valeri; p. 52, Raff Frano; pp. 54, 58, 60, Buffalo Bills, Robert L. Smith Photography; p. 62, Cleveland Browns, Inc., Henry M. Barr Studios, Inc., pp. 75, 76, 78, New York Jets.

Cover photograph: Thomas J. Croke, New England Patriots

80